The Weary
Soul
He Holds

Blessitt Johnson

Contents

The Weary Soul He Holds

The Weary Soul He Holds

Discarded But Not Abandoned

Discarded yet not abandoned,
Tossed to the wayside but found by the waymaker.
Left without care yet still cared for.
A thoughtless being no longer of importance-
yet he thought enough to think of me.
An unwanted trinket thrown out,
but it was a golden treasure in his eyes.
The last of the last in their heads,
yet the first choice he chose.
Something that can't be explained.

Discarded yet not abandoned,
broken but not shattered.
A child begging for bread,
and he fed me until I was full.
Babes in need of nourishment,
yet he supplied milk and honey.
Forgotten by earthly caretakers,
but never forsaken by the Creator.
He saw the abandonment, He bore our pain,
He saw our wounds and heard prayers-
The maker of all things has not abandoned us.

The Weary Soul He Holds

Discarded but not abandoned,
beaten but no bruise.
Hurting but he heals every wound.
God will never leave us or forsake us-
The promise was marked at the cross.
An orphan with no mother,
but a heavenly father who cared.
Invisible to them,
but seen in Him.
An old love that was lost,
yet another love gained.

The Everglades

My life was like the Everglades,
wild and endangered.
Made to display beauty,
but was full of hard-hearted reflections and
hazardous waste.
Chained by the wilderness of regret and sin,
but He freed me from it all and more.
Drowning in a swamp of questions I wanted to ask
you, but instead, He answered me.
He turned my Everglade into a beautiful reservoir
only He could fill.

Jeremiah 31:25

*All the nights where I laid awake unable to sleep,
while my weary heart wished you would answer.
All the times I felt such deep sorrow from the trials
I faced, wondering where my joy went.
Then suddenly you reminded me that you give rest
to the weary and overwhelming joy to those filled
with sorrow.
When the pain begins to cut too deep you bandage
the wounds quickly.
When the waters began to rise too close to my neck,
you brought them back down again.
Your love goes beyond the depths of man's love.
Your loving care cannot be matched!*

Scotland Hills

Dune hills that look like mountains
that oversee the valley below.
A land beautifully crafted by the master crafter
and an ocean that flows.
He's the God of the mountaintop and the valley
below.
The beauty of Scotland Hills.
Where the sun peaks between the land
and the sky.
Grassy trails that lead to unknown adventures
and mysteries.

Scotland Hills reminds me of how Jesus departed
to pray to the Father.
Where peace meets at the center, its trees aged over
time but bloomed beautifully
and its castles stand tall like giants.
Where rivers flow and clouds glide across
the sky.
It is God's craftsmanship.

Igloos

Tried to guard my heart but instead, it became an
igloo.
Hard and walled up so no one could get in,
but somehow you found a way.
Now I'm left picking up blocks of ice that were
destroyed and melted.
Don't harden your heart, My child, you said.
But I refused.
Igloo after igloo and tear after tear.
He reminds me of his love.

Separate But Not Alone

Separate but not alone.
Set aside but not disowned.
The same but changed.
Rejected by them but accepted
by Him.
Separated but not alone.
Dwelling here but not home.
Tossed away by others but
reeled in by The One.

Not lonely but separated
Not punishment but restoration.
Not losing but winning favor.
A plan panned out.
A story being written.
Humble submission is not worthless
worldly attention.

Wildflowers

We were like wildflowers dancing in the wind.
Not planted by man's hand but from his.
We bloomed on fertile soil and grew on good
ground.
We quietly whistled in the wind
and did not make a sound.

Caged Heart

Here lie the pieces of my heart barred behind this
cage.
I am numbed by all of life's reckoning.
Was handed the key but refused to unlock the door
to my bondage.

Open your heart again
Don't you dare throw away the keys
I am here saying" Come to me all who are weary
and have heavy burdens."
But I failed to comply.

I've made skepticism a bed and fear a blanket.
I will not be hurt again.
A caged heart he did not create.
A broken spirit but he is close.

They See Unfixable But God Sees Different

When they look at me they see an unfixable
situation and a lost cause but God sees differently.
He sees you healed, he sees you free.
He sees you happy, and joyful, being who you're
made to be.

When people saw a dead girl, he saw her asleep.
When people saw a shepherd boy, he saw a king.
And when people saw a closed tomb, he saw a
different scene.

He is the fixer of all fixers and a God who knows
what to do.
The unfixable becomes fixable and the old becomes
new.

Bird On The Ledge

Like a bird on a ledge, there I sat all alone.
Thinking too deeply about my life and how I did not
fit.
I flew with different groups and hung out with
many crowds.
But I felt like I did not exist.
Like a bird on a ledge, I sat in solitude.
Reminding myself that I was a puzzle with a
missing piece and a plant with no water to survive.

At that ledge, I was reminded of my need for you.
You were that missing piece …
                         of the puzzle that is.
So I chose to choose you.

Love

Love is patient and Love is kind.
It is rare, it is golden and very hard to find.
But there is one person whose love is real.
The love of the Father is a pretty big deal.

His love is not like man's, he does not fail or
disappoint.
He loves with mercy, he loves as he protects.
He strengthens us when we are weak and when we
are wrecked.

His timing is perfect and his time is right.
So be patient and don't put up a fight.
The love he brings will be like a freshwater spring.
It is a love that will last forever.

Eagle's Wings

All our lives we would run but grow weary, and
would walk but faint.
We spent our lives trusting in fantasies and earthly
vanities that could not heal.
Gave our attention to false gods and false
perceptions that were not real.
That caused us to drown in a pit of our own grief.

Dug holes in our graves, and paved a path we
should not have paved,
only to not soar in the end.
But when you trust in the Lord and refuse to
entertain what he did not send.
You will soar on an eagle's wings.
Thrive in every area and everything.
        Win and not lose…
            You'll be guided and not confused…
Because those who put their hope in the Lord will
renew their strength.

Trenches

From cold nights to tireless days.
The trenches are where we were raised.
Where shoes hung on electric poles, and graffiti was
plastered on every corner.
Where making ends meet seemed impossible and
breaking bread was scarce.
Where flowers bloomed but our hearts did not.
Where love died but hatred was hot.

The trenches gave no hope.
But as we sat in those pews and heard those words,
" Jesus loves us ".
We wondered if it was true.
There was no love where we reside, yet he was a
God that sees all.
 So we could not run and we could not hide.

The Pier

I step along this Pier gazing upon the water's edge.
I admire the view.
As time passes I think of you and I ask…
Why us?
Why now?
Why this?
Too many questions but not enough answers.

At that Pier, I realized the cold truth…
That this world grows strangely dim and
earthly treasures do fade.
I glanced for a moment at the trees and noticed how
they were constantly at worship.
So I question why aren't we?

That Pier suddenly became my new view and an
eye-opener
to see.
But what you might ask…?
A new perspective and a new scene.

Fear To Fail

One fall, one trip, and you out
A thought that rewinds in my head.
The fear of failure, how terrible it must be.
To see everything you dreamed of fall before your
feet.
But don't be afraid and don't you fret.
You might fail but it's not over yet.
For God has a purpose, a plan, and a will.
So sit back and relax and please be still.

Who I Thought You Were

You showed me who I thought you were,
 but he showed me who you are.
Young and naive.
Had eyes but could not see.
But now my eyes are open and
I can see the truth.
So I will not turn back to what I once knew.

A Rare Flower

You are RARE.
A one-of-a-lifetime thing.
A rare plant sitting in an open field.
Rare flowers don't compare and rare flowers don't
compete.
Remember this love.

The one that waters you, sees your uniqueness.
He sees your delicacy.
There is no need for envy or jealousy because you
are one of a kind.
A perfectly potted gift that won't be missed but
seen.

A rare flower that deserves the best gardener at its
side.
So don't think for a minute that you aren't enough.

Little Girl on the Pavement

A little girl with a flower in her hand,
and a flower in her hair as she stares at the
pavement wondering where she'll go next.
She's journeyed from home to home,
and from place to place.
Yet there's still no space for her.

She weeps and pouts with her chubby cheeks,
as she waits and waits to be held.
Just a little girl on the pavement, waiting for all to
be well but peace has not found her yet.

Don't worry little child, don't you fret, the creator of
all things is not done yet.
He cares for the widows and the orphaned ones.
Yes.. he does indeed.
He'll place you in a loving family, just wait and see.
The petals from your flowers have caught his
attention, and he has heard your cries.
You are no longer a child on the Pavement but a
daughter of the most high.

When The Leaves Fall

In his eyes, we are like trees planted with good
seeds.
We were made to let our branches grow and our
leaves bloom.
The seasons change and so do we.
First, we're tall and green and then we lose all our
leaves.

What do you do when the leaves fall?
What do you do when there seems to be no hope at
all?
What do you do when you are bare and life seems
not fair?

When the leaves fall and the gardener begins to
prune.
Just know that you're on your way to a better you.
God cuts and prunes to improve and reuse.

The Nestrians

Like Nestrians we didn't fit in.
Tossed aside like worthless treasures.
We were outcasts among the great and
hated by the elites.
We shone bright in the darkness and glowed
with radiant joy.
We failed to blend in but the truth is..their destiny
was not ours.
And their remarks were not the final say.
We were created by the Creator to bring light.
While their lights were dimmed, we were bright.
When storms raged we were made to swim
not sink.
We were made to thrive, not hide.
Made to encourage them not to die.
Made to stand beyond our hearts
breaking the brink.

Doubt Is A Dangerous Disease

Doubt is a dangerous disease.
It feeds on things that are not true.
It plagues your mind and divides your time and
energy away from the one that made you.
The wait is long but worth it.
So don't doubt the plan or purpose.

Maine

Maine is a beautiful place.
4,000 islands off the coast of this space and
32,000 miles of rivers and streams.
But what could this mean?

It means that God is an artist not just a way maker.
Not just a burden taker.
Not just a life-changing orchestrator.
But an artist with a brush.

I wish to reside in Maine where Portland's
lighthouse is because it reminds me of your light.
I wish to sit in the grass and stare out into the
open..in silence, not a word being spoken.
I wish to stare up at the sky as the sun and clouds as
they begin to connect.
It reminds me that you're here.
It reminds me not to fear.
It reminds me to focus and to remember that I am
chosen.

Thorns In My Side

There are thorns in my side and holes in my hands
from life's chaotic demise.
Each splinter made me remember just how bad it
must be to see what this ugly sin has done.
The aches that come from tragedy and the pain that
comes from the hell of this world have
made me weak.

This pain hurts! This pain it grieves!
It is too much to bear.
Can you please take it away ..!
Can you please just close the wound..!

The thorns in our sides make us feel like we've been
left to die and this is our punishment.
But the truth is we are not

The same thorns in my side are in his and the same
holes in my hands are in his… only his are truly
REAL.

Because he is the ONE who paid the PRIC**E.**
Day by day we scream, "Father why have you
forsaken me?

Burden Bearer

The burdens we carry can be painful and scary but they do not stand toe to toe with God.
When turmoil devours our souls and grief grabs hold of our hearts.
 He is our burden taker.
The burdens we bear and the despair that is laid upon our backs will soon turn into ashes of dust never to be seen again.

Cold Callouses

Like cold callouses we are hard-headed, he supplies
water but yet we are dry.
He brings relief but yet we would rather die of a
cold heart.
The brokenness of our hearts has awoken him to act
on our behalf.
We are put last by mere men and mistreated by
savages.
I know that it hurts but trust this one thing.
The first shall be last and the last shall be first.
So don't let others count you out.
And don't follow in their footsteps concerning your
heart posture.
Because he takes a cold callous and turns it into a
soft bed of skin.
By killing the sin within.

The Day I Lost You

One day you were here and now you're not.
One day I was admiring your smile but now you are
gone.
No one knows God's divine appointments.
No one knows his divine times.
The grievance of a loved one.
The loss of a friend and a pain that cuts deep.
The day I lost you, truly made me weep.
But eventually, birds die and flowers wither.
And so do we.
When we grieve, God grieves.
So you're not alone.

This Here Cell

In this cell, I'm left thinking... What now?
Behind those bars, I see millions
of souls that bleed for a missing deity.
Bodies that lay down at night asleep but dead.
Hungry souls needed to be fed.
Though they are locked up, there is a God who
provides freedom.
And though they see darkness, he is their light.
Because even though they kill the body, they cannot
kill the soul.
Because God is faithful and he is true.
He comes to love, correct, and save you.

Psalm 23:4

You've walked through the darkest valleys and felt the breath of death, yet you still survived.
You've tasted a pinch of fear and walked on dry bones, yet it did not overtake you.

For he provides green pastures and his rod and staff comfort you.
He restores your aching soul and leads you to still water.
He shepherds you like a lamb who needs a guide.
Because surely his goodness and mercy follow.

When the valley of death called "Life" begins to appear.
DO NOT FEAR!
Your pastures of peace have arrived and your table has been prepared.
You shall not want a thing.

Disappointment

Dear disappointment,
Who knew you'd come this quick?
I've done my best to suppress every part of you.
A fourteen-letter word that grows bigger with time.
I cry for relief that seems so far away…
I soon begin to doubt but God reminds me that,
"When the righteous cry" , he answers.
When in trouble he delivers.

Where The Sun Sets At

Catch me where the sun sets.
Where I sit and admire the sky from every range.
Catch me where the sun sets.
Where glimpses of his handy work lie.
Where pastures of green grass and land are not too
hard to find.
Catch me gazing upon his glory.
Where every part of the earth connects so perfectly.
Suddenly my worries leave me and my fears fly
quickly.
Because the sunset is where I get my relief.

Look Again

It looks like you've lost
It looks like they won, but please look again.
Vindication has been set and justice will prevail.
After all, I know you've been through hell.
But please look again.

Look at what I am doing.
Look at what I have done.
I know every scar and everything under the sun.
I am doing a new thing
Can't you see?
You're about to take off.
Into new heights and new beginnings.

Roses of Betrayal

A bouquet of roses that expresses my love for you
ended up being the weapon to my greatest betrayal.
Who knew that your bittersweet kisses could
feel like bullets to my soul?
The petals you laid and the love you gave left me
with tears.
These roses of betrayal are what made me
cold but he restored me to my natural self.
A beautiful flower he created became a glimpse of
the pieces of my heart.
But he arose and made it whole again.

Galatians 6:9

Please don't grow weary in doing good because
your reward is coming soon.
Don't give up in the waiting because you're getting
ready to bloom.
The road is tough and the way can get ugly but
don't you dare give in.
Because God doesn't take L's.
It's always a win-win.

Heal

Heal while there's time. Heal in this space.
Take your time and run at your own pace.
If you do not heal, you'll continue to spill on
those who did not hurt you.

Move and adjust. Have patience and trust,
 that God can heal your wounds.
No scar is too deep and no pain is too strong for
God.
Is anything too hard for him..?
Certainly not.

Dover

Grassy cliffs and beautiful hills.
The view of Dover is like staring at the art of God's
hand within a masterpiece.
From the blue waters to the clear skies,
a physical picture of peace and serenity.
Lord make me like Dover, England
Beautiful but humble.
Shines loud but is so peaceful.

A place where you sit at the edge of cliffs,
admiring the new perspective God gave.
Where blue waters remind you of the way,
Jesus walked them gracefully.
The way its stillness reminds you that you're
not in control but God is.

Knives That Cut Deep

I've got knives that cut deep in the depths of my
back but yet I still stand.
I will not die because I know who lives.
I will not lose because I know who wins.
I will not quit because I know who started it all.

Though I bleed, I am strong.
Though I weep, my tears are wiped away.
Count the cost, add up the change, and
see for yourself if this is where you want to be.

I am a sheep to the slaughter and prey for the
hunter.
I am a martyr of righteousness and a threat to what
they disown.
I've got knives in my back from those who don't
know the truth.
So they slay me.

Don't Look Back

Don't look back but look ahead to what God's doing
next.
Prepare, and rest knowing you've passed the test.
Don't be like Lot's wife.
Don't mourn over what's old.
But leave it in the dust to rot, rust, and mold.

Don't fall for the familiar
Don't desire its taste.
Don't look back, it will be a waste.
Keep on running, keep on the move.
Because the promise is on the horizon and so is a
breakthrough.

The Wilderness Of Job

It was no man's land where we reside.
Had only enough to get by.
Went from being on the mountaintop to sitting in
deserts of ruin.
Our anguish was no good for us and our longing for
peace became rubbish.
Yet we did not understand why this happened to us.

We were people of integrity and we carried
ourselves gracefully but that did not stop this trial.
Soon we wondered if death was a better fate.
Then we noticed that this was a test that came with
a mess…
        that would soon be cleared.
God had faith in us when we did not.
The devil had hoped that we would rot,
but yet we live.

In Time

In time, we will dine with the one who sets the
table.
Soon we will discover that all our grief and turmoil
was only a season
and the reason behind the mess.
In time tears will be gone and the heart will be
mended.
In time you'll heal and you won't feel what you once
felt.

His timing.
    Our patience.

The Moment I Knew

I stopped, took a deep breath, and realized this was
the moment I knew.
This chapter was closed and this part of the story
 was coming to an end yet I fear the new me.
I fear what I did not know.
This was when I knew that trusting in God came
without borders and required me to walk on waters I
thought I would sink in.

Ties That Bind

The ties that bind us together come from trauma and
stress.
We connected through our infected perceptions of
life.
Our hidden bruises and excuses kept us close but
little did we know we were poisoned to each other.
From soul ties to the trauma bonds, it was our fatal
destruction.
But HE was our rescuer.
He was the reason why the ties were cut.
A blessing in disguise and a peace I never knew.

Cold Nights

Late in the midnight hours when the earth is still.
My mind spirals with thoughts that I cannot
understand.
My mind deepens by the hour and my heart begins
to fail.
All the memories and wasted energy seem to arise
and appear.
But YOU were there in those cold nights and there
to catch every tear.
You gave me warmth when I was cold and numb,
and renewal when my mind was wrecked.

Counted Me Out

I counted myself out and threw away the key to the
things that made me great.
But I cannot quit.
People are counting on me to be everything that
you've created me to be...
Yet I still doubt my potential here.

Beauty In The Ashes

Out of the ashes, there is beauty.
A hard thing to believe when your life becomes
shambles and your heart becomes weak.
But he makes a mess into a masterpiece, a test into a
testimony, and pain into purpose in the blink of an
eye.
From dust to dawn and ashes to light.
God makes something out of nothing.

Maui

Walking these shores became the cure to my soul.
These palm trees and rushing seas began to overtake
me.
My feet in the sand and shells in my hand made me
appreciate the little things in life.
There I sat in Maui looking at a land I did not know
but it felt like home.
The tips of your pen and the paint from your brush
created something so beautiful.
Suddenly tears leave and anxiety fades into the
distance.

Closer Than A Brother

Friends come and go but whoever stays.
They appear, laugh, and then fade away but who
sticks closer than a brother?
When it pours and rains, who is standing tall?
When you are down and you fall, who is there
through it all?
Is there even just one?

    A risky commitment.
A joining and a cling.
    A sacrificial love that goes beyond and above.
Something so hard to find.
But one thing we forget and another we fret.
That HE has been one from the start.
A father, a friend, and a love that never falls apart.

Psalm 38:8

I sat at the edge of anguish as this heavy burden of
affliction has broken me.
My misery has seeped through my bones.
I gasp for relief but they say there is none but God
reminds me that he's there.
So I plead for my deliverance from this place.

Blurred Validation

Like celebrities, we crave the attention of men
and the idea of fans.
   A blurred validation.
   A deadly demise.
Trying to feed the starvation of the void in our souls
that can only be filled by **HIM.**

Where Our Hearts Lie

Too often our hearts lie in desert places and
hopeless spaces that bring us no joy.
But he gave us another way...
Not fame or fortune or anything in vain but in Him.
When our hearts lie there, they are safe...
When our hearts lie there they race.
When our hearts lie there we are full of satisfaction.

Window Seal

Here I sit at this window seal watching as the
blazing sun bursts through the room.
The walls were its canvas, as it lightened up this
darkened gloom.
All the tears I cried hid behind the seams and in
between the blinds.
But God's light met me at the window seal.
Where I wondered what now and why.

The Girl In The Wheat Field

I see a vision of a field.
A short glimpse of a girl running through the wheat.
As she twists and twirls her smile can not be beat.
She flows in the wind as the sun hits her face
causing her to glow.
I stopped only to see that this girl was me.

Her posture resembled peace and her smile spoke of
freedom.
A representation of death to life.
From bondage to free.
A short glimpse of the woman I'll soon be.

The Girl in the Wheat Field.

The Gulf

My heart was like the gulf's water that raged in the
wind.
My emotions bordered at the coastlines of doubt
and fear.
My hope sank deep into the depths of the sea's
floor.
Overwhelmed by bodies of water filled with stress,
and shores of sinking plans.
He was the lifeboat I needed to survive and an
anchor I needed so I could not move.
He calms my heart's gulf by saying" Peace be still."

The Ark Promise

In my darkness your light shines.
When I felt unworthy you reminded me of your
promises.
The same promise that shined as **Noah** left the **ark.**
A sheer sign to us today.
That glorious **rainbow**.
That wonderful sign.
I'll keep it close to my heart when I lose my way.
You promised to return to rescue us so I'll continue
to hope for that glorious day.
The Ark promise you made!

I See God

I see God in the everyday conversations
 and the mundane things.
I see God and his love in the streets, in alleys, on
bridges,
        and near streams.
He gives assurance to those who trust in Him
wholeheartedly.
Don't you see?

He's there at the lake
He's there at home
He's in your heart and inside your bones.
Can you see Him, my friend?
He's not just in one place but in every corner and
every space.
I see God in the ups
I see God in the downs.
    He's there in our grief.
            He's there in our hurt.
He promised that he would never desert us.

I SEE GOD
Don't you? My friend.
He promised to be with us until the end.

Clouds

White clouds and blue skies.
I stare at the painting you painted.
I imagine you there sitting by my side reminding
me not to fear.
I long to finally be there with you, but there is
much work for me to still do.
So I'll continue to chase the clouds waiting
for you.

The Butterfly Effect

From a lovely caterpillar squirming on a leaf to a
beautiful butterfly breaking forth from a cocoon.
We transition from old to new.
It's an effect. The butterfly one that is.
God puts us on a firm foundation and plants us on
fertile soil so that our branches bloom.
He prepared the way because his son would come
soon.
We are beautiful butterflies waiting to burst and
trees that transform into cypresses.

Empty Cup

You spend days on end going above and beyond for
those who do not choose you.
You pour into cups that leave you empty so tell me
who fills you?
You fight for those who do not fight for you and
you care for others who do not care about you?
So tell me who takes care of you?
You cross oceans for people who would not cross
them for you.
So you're left gasping for air.
The water that filled you was used to fill others not
realizing that this would leave you dry.
Now you are left admiring an empty cup of a soul
that used to be full…

                    but is now dead.

Psalm 102

In my distress, I sought your face pleading in grief.
I yelled at you for help from those who opposed me.
When they sought to destroy my life and erase my
existence, I wondered if you were watching from a
distance.
When their mockeries and monitoring stockers
prolonged, I wept tears of bitter pain.
I questioned your silence which angered me.
Do you not see what they have done?
Do you not see what I see?
Suddenly silence broke and an answer rained from
the sky.
You incline your ears to hear me as I bend on my
knees, reminding me that you did not pass me by.

Rest

This was an exhaustion that came with insomnia
that left me snoozing and pain that left me with a
bruise.
It was like torture to see myself fading into the
distance while my heart began to sink.
Time after time I spent depriving myself of sleep
while medicating my wounds with melodies.
Suddenly you whispered words so heavenly to my
ears saying, "Please just rest" but I declined.

Tidal Waves

Like tidal waves, the tears came rushing in from the
fear I felt.
I sat stiffly on the ground and looked at my
reflection that mirrored through the water.
Desperately I look up at the stars realizing your
presence there.
Quickly my tears fade.

Dancing On Daisies

From the porch to the riverbanks will be dancing on
daisies of what he did.
We'll be gliding through fields and leaping through
the air because God's joy has filled our souls.
We transition from sad to glad, defeat to victory,
and from broken songs into symphonies.
We'll be dancing on Daisies in the promised land.
Looking at prayers bloom from our tears.

I Survived

Beneath the rubble of jealousy and the pile of ridicule, I survived.
Underneath the crushing weight of pain and the blisters of depression, I rise.
My enemies wanted me to die yet I lived.
They sought to break me yet I was unbreakable so they watched in confusion.
Thrown into a pit with no regard for saving me yet I still made it out on top.
Their evil plans were the rubber band that launched me to the palace.

1 Out Of The 99

Out of all the herd he came and found me, the one
who lost his way.
Had many sheep to tend but he decided to spend a
little extra time with me.
When I went left he made me right.
When I gave up he chose to fight.
His love would not quit.
The heavens rejoiced when I returned home.

Psalm 109:31

When weak and needy you stand beside me.
When I break beyond broken you mend the pieces.
When they condemn me, you stand ready to defend.
When they persecute, you come to my rescue time
and time again.

Vivid Reality

This life I was living seemed real but soon I realized
it was just a dream.
Where feelings did not exist and hearts did not
break.
A dream so vivid but not true.
In reality, my emotions and physicality screamed
for relief from this place.
I lay asleep wishing I could stay in this realistic
fantasy for a lifetime but morning broke and God
awoke me.

Bare Oak Trees

I was a plant with no leaves looking lifeless and
cold.
Bare and hollow
Plain but unique.
Brittle but still able to stand.
I thought my life was meaningless, a story with no
intent of a happy ending.
Yet you turned my bareness into fruitfulness with
one touch.
 Your tender loving care caused me to grow and my
leaves to finally bloom.

Thick of The Mud

In the thick of the mud you pulled me out.
When stains paint my clothes you make them
stainless.
All while I doubted if I would ever be clean.
This ugly sin was hideous on me but I feared that it
was too great...
    Yet you advise me that you're greater.

Ocean Road, Australia

A jaw-dropping coastline and a rugged beauty you cannot miss.
A sight I truly wish to see.
Its dirt roads lead to crystal blue waters and rocky shores.
A place where solitude took its course and tranquility breathed.
It's where memories leave and heartaches wither.
A place where talking to God seemed to come easy and comfort followed not too far behind.

Pillar Of Salt

Like Lot's wife I found myself mourning over
something I did not need which caused me to turn
into a pillar of salt.
Stiff and unable to move I panicked at the thought
of it.
Regretting my way of thinking, I pleaded to be free.
    But my mind would not quit.
So I grieve internally for you quietly and you heard
me.

Cherry Blossoms

I sat daydreaming about the cherry blossoms and
how their vibrant appearance and beautiful flow
made me wish I was in Japan.
I imagine walking down that long road that leads to
a trail of its petals before ever reaching its full view.
Gasping in amazement at what I see.
Eager to escape my pain I visualize what it would
be like to admire this masterpiece God made.
A calming assurance and resting peace.

This Is Not The End

We look at our situation and we question "Is this the
end?"
Because deep in our hearts crave better results yet
he reminds us that this is not the end.
The grief won't last and depression will fade.
The hurt will heal and the heart won't rage.
Pain will soon be no more.

This is not the end…

    A sentence too good to be true.

You See Me

All my life I crumbled under the weight of feeling non-existent.
Visible to the public eye but still not seen.
Like an outcast, I just knew I didn't belong..
But you reminded me that you love those who sojourner, and need your comfort when no one else is near.
When they fail to see, you see…**ME.**

For this, I am forever grateful.

About The Author

The author, **Blessitt Johnson,** born in 1999 is a writer and poet.
As a small-town girl in the heart of east Texas, after countless attempts to pursue a college degree and wondering where her future would go. She trusted God and years later pursued her passion of writing poetry books for those who struggle with mental health such as anxiety, depression, and loneliness just like her. While showing others how God is in every situation and every circumstance.

She also enjoys writing books that discuss real-life issues such as abandonment, trauma, and abuse. Blessitt spends most of her time at home with family and friends, going to the park, and traveling. For more information about upcoming books, questions or concerns contact johnsonblessitt57@gmail.com.

The Weary Soul He Holds

Milton Keynes UK
Ingram Content Group UK Ltd.
UKHW030813130224
437765UK00014B/501